BARE ROOT
Sweets

30 Paleo Dessert Recipes for the Modern Food Lover
RECIPES & PHOTOGRAPHY BY ANGELA GALLARDO

First Edition 2013
ISBN (paperback) 978-1-4928-5827-0

CONTENTS

ABOUT BARE ROOT

BareRootGirl.com and the Bare Root cookbooks are an endeavor to unite the modern food lover in me with my primally passionate side.

I'd built my cooking knowledge base via a Food Network addiction and struggled for years to reconcile my love of good food with my desire to be health conscious. I'd come to believe it was an impossible feat.

My awareness of the Paleo/Primal lifestyle came about slowly. Naturally, at first, I felt it was far too limiting to really let my passion for flavor flourish and I brushed it aside. But I was pulled toward the natural foundations of the diet, the modern application of an ancestral way of life. Eliminating all the processed junk and adapting a more simplistic approach toward eating felt instinctual to me. And it ultimately overruled my desire for what I considered at the time to be 'fine foods.'

Like many others, a number of life circumstances regarding my own suffering health gradually pushed me further down the Paleo/Primal path. I learned that ultimately this lifestyle is really about replacing nutrient poor foods with nutrient dense foods. It's not about subscribing religiously to a Paleo dogma or creating lists of 'ok' and 'not ok' foods. It's about eliminating those foods that research now tells us are harmful to our bodies (like grains, legumes, and sugar) and incorporating foods that our bodies respond well to based on personal experience. I believe whole-heartedly that every individual can find a Paleo model that works for themselves and that it can cure many of the ailments plaguing our society today.

I started BareRootGirl.com to challenge myself to create recipes that were not just delicious but nutrient dense, as well. At times, it can be frustrating to work without so many of the staples I was used to growing up. But it's exhilarating, and very rewarding, to create nutritious meals free of disease-causing anti-nutrients.

INTRO TO BARE ROOT SWEETS

The positive response I've received on BareRootGirl.com motivated me to begin a collection of cookbooks (available in both e-copy and paperback) that will serve as inspiration for others to unite a Paleo/Primal diet with modern 'fine food' eating.

Quality ingredients promote maximum flavor in every recipe included here. Everything from investigating the proper handling of raw ingredients to the precisely lowest amount of sweetener a recipe needs to be appealing were given a great deal of consideration. And because food is truly lovely, I tried to let the finished products shine in their natural beauty as much as possible.

It should be addressed that we know our ancestors weren't munching on dark chocolate truffles or coconut milk cheesecakes. But the approach I've taken with these recipes (and the ingredients they contain) reflects back to my personal approach to the lifestyle, which is focusing on the nutrient density of the ingredients.

Truth be told, desserts should not be a daily occurrence in a Paleo/Primal diet. For many, not even a weekly occurrence. But an essential part of moving over to this way of eating has been affording myself the occasional treat. And over time, my tastes have changed and I've learned that I don't need nearly the amount of sweetness I used to think was a requirement in desserts.

I've made an effort to include many sugar-free dessert options that will still satiate your sweet tooth. My go-to Date Paste recipe works as a great sweetener and is noted in the recipes where it works well as a replacement. Additionally, there are a few recipes that can be made without any sweetener at all, if you're on a 21DSD or simply wanting a guilt-free treat!

All recipes are 100% original creations. And as many of them took quite a number of attempts to perfect, I'm extremely excited for you to try them.

CAKES

9 No-Bake Pumpkin Cheesecake

10 Lemony Angel Food Cake

13 Spiced Peach Buckle

14 Banana & Caraway Pound Cake

15 Chocolatey Cacao Cupcakes

16 Chai-Spiced Carrot Cake

NO-BAKE PUMPKIN CHEESECAKE

Ginger Crust

2 c.	raw walnuts
3	dried medjool dates
2 t.	ground ginger
1/2 t.	sea salt
2 T.	blackstrap molasses
1/4 c.	grass-fed butter or virgin coconut

Cheesecake Filling

2	lemons, juice (warmed)
1 T.	grass-fed gelatin
2 c.	Cultured Coconut "Cream Cheese"
1 can	organic full-fat coconut milk
1/2 c.	organic grade B maple syrup (or 1 c. Date Paste, pg. 40)
1	vanilla bean
1 t.	vanilla extract
1/2 t.	sea salt

Pumpkin Topping

1 can	organic pumpkin puree (15 oz)
1/4 c.	organic grade B maple syrup (or 1/2 c. Date Paste, pg. 40)
1	lemon, juiced
1 t.	vanilla extract
1 t.	ground cinnamon
1/8 t.	ground cloves
1/4 t.	sea salt
2 t.	tapioca starch

A creamy, no-bake dessert with a little fall flavor. Make your own coconut "cream cheese" for that traditional tang or substitute plain coconut cream.

Directions:

1. *Make the crust*: place all crust ingredients into the bowl of a large food processor. Process until mixture is combined well, scraping the sides down occasionally. Press into a 9-inch spring form pan and refrigerate 30+ minutes.

2. *Make the filling*: mix warmed lemon juice and gelatin in a small bowl until gelatin is dissolved. Set aside.

3. Combine remaining filling ingredients in the bowl of a large food processor and process until smooth, about 30-60 seconds. With the food processor running, slowly drizzle in warm lemon juice/gelatin mixture and process to combine, another 30 seconds. Pour filling into chilled Ginger Crust and refrigerate 1-2 hours.

4. *Make the topping*: combine all topping ingredients in a blender. Blend on high until smooth, about 30-60 seconds. Pour into a small saucepan and heat until mixture begins to bubble.

5. Pour Pumpkin Topping over chilled crust/filling and serve. Or place back in refrigerator minimum 8 hours for a more set-up presentation.

Cultured Coconut "Cream Cheese"

Yields:	2 cups
2 c.	organic coconut cream
1	probiotic capsule (or approx. 30 mil active cultures)

1. *Prepare "Cream Cheese" ahead*: place coconut cream in a strainer lined with tea towel or cheesecloth. Place strainer over a large bowl to catch coconut water. Let sit 1+ hours. Wrap the tea towel around the cream and squeeze out any remaining coconut water.

2. Move coconut cream to a glass pint jar, open the probiotic capsule, and mix in granules well. Screw a lid on tightly and place the jar in the oven with the oven light on (the heat from the light will allow the coconut cream to culture). Leave minimum 12 hours or longer to intensify the "cream cheese" sourness. Store in fridge.

> *This cake gets its airy texture from a batter of egg whites whipped into a stiff meringue. Hibiscus-infused cherries add a tart, sweetly floral flavor.*

Angel Food Cake

12	pastured egg whites
2.3 c.	raw honey
1/2	lemon, juiced
1/2 t.	sea salt
1 T.	vanilla extract
1/3 c.	organic coconut flour
3/4 c.	tapioca starch
1	lemon, zest

Lemon Cream Frosting

1 1/3 c.	organic coconut cream
2 T.	virgin coconut oil
1	lemon, juice & zest
1 T.	raw honey
2 T.	grass-fed gelatin
pinch	sea salt

Hibiscus Cherries

1/2 c.	dried hibiscus flowers
1/2	lemon, juiced
1 T.	raw honey
pinch	sea salt
1 c.	fresh cherries, halved

Angel Food Cake Directions:

1. Preheat oven to 350F. Combine egg whites, honey, lemon juice, and sea salt in the bowl of a stand mixer. Place the bowl over a bowl of hot water simmering on medium-low heat. Whisk continuously until honey is melted and eggs feel warm to the touch.

2. Transfer the bowl to a stand mixer fitted with a whisk attachment. Beat on medium speed 30 seconds, increase speed to medium high for another 30 seconds, then move to high speed for 2-3 minutes, or until mixture has doubled in volume and formed a stiff meringue. Add vanilla extract and mix on high another 30 seconds.

3. In a separate bowl, whisk together coconut flour, tapioca starch, and lemon zest. Sift mixture in thirds into the meringue, gently folding it in with a spatula, careful not to deflate the egg whites too much.

4. Scoop and smooth batter into an angel food cake pan. Tap the pan on the counter to remove air bubbles. Bake 40 min, or until golden brown and a skewer comes out clean. Invert to cool 2+ hours before frosting and serving.

Lemon Cream Frosting Directions:

1. Combine ingredients in the top bowl of a double boiler. Whisk until mixture is fully combined and gelatin is melted. Move to the refrigerator and chill 1 hour.

2. Transfer chilled mixture to the bowl of a stand mixer fitted with a whisk attachment. Whisk on high until mixture doubles in volume, about 2-3 minutes. Spread onto cake immediately (it will set up quickly).

Hibiscus Cherries Directions:

1. In a small saucepan, combine hibiscus with 1 cup of water. Cook to a simmer over medium heat. Remove from heat, cover with lid, and let steep for 10 minutes.

2. Strain out hibiscus flowers and place the liquid back into the saucepan. Mix in honey and lemon juice and bring to a simmer over medium heat. Cook to reduce by half, about 5-10 minutes. Add cherries and a pinch of sea salt. Remove from heat and allow to cool to room temperature before topping the cake.

LEMONY ANGEL FOOD CAKE
with lemon cream & hibiscus cherries

SPICED PEACH BUCKLE

buck·le (bŭk'əl)

noun.
1. a traditional, cake-like batter layered underneath fruit.
2. the cake rises around the fruit, which tries its best to sink to the bottom, making the whole thing buckle inwards.

Ingredients

3	pastured eggs	1/4 t.	baking soda
1/2 c.	organic coconut milk	1/2 t.	sea salt
1 T.	virgin coconut oil	2	ripe peaches
1/2 c.	Date Paste (pg. 40)	1	lemon, juiced
1 t.	vanilla extract	1 T.	ground cinnamon
1/3 c.	organic coconut flour	1/4 t.	ground ginger
1 T.	ground flaxseed	1/4 t.	freshly ground nutmeg
1/2 t.	baking powder	1 T.	virgin coconut oil, for greasing

1. Preheat oven to 350F.

2. In a small bowl, combine peach slices, lemon juice, cinnamon, ginger, and nutmeg. Toss well to coat and set aside.

3. In the bowl of a stand mixer, mix eggs, coconut milk, coconut oil, date paste, and vanilla on medium speed until combined. Add coconut flour, flaxseed, baking powder, baking soda, and sea salt. Mix on medium high speed until mixture is smooth and no lumps are apparent.

4. Place the melted coconut oil in the bottom of an 8 x 8" baking pan. Pour the coconut flour batter mixture on top of the oil and gently spread to coat the bottom. Arrange the peach slices one by one, creating 2 even rows in the batter (as shown in the picture).

5. Bake for 40-50 minutes, or until center is set and top is golden brown. Serve warm as-is or topped with coconut milk.

BANANA CARAWAY POUND CAKE

1 c.	grass-fed butter, softened	3/4 c.	organic coconut flour
1/2-1 c.	organic coconut sugar (optional)	1 t.	baking powder
3	pastured eggs, room temperature	1/2 t.	baking soda
3	bananas, mashed	2 T.	caraway seeds
2 T.	organic full-fat coconut milk	1 t.	sea salt
2 t.	vanilla extract	1 t.	nigella seeds (optional)

> *A sweet, buttery loaf flavored with aromatic caraway. Top with peppery nigella seeds for a uniquely savory cake.*

Directions:

1. Preheat oven to 350F. Grease a 4 1/2 x 8 1/2 loaf pan. Toast caraway seeds in a dry sauté pan for 3-5 minutes, or until fragrant. Set aside to cool.
2. Combine butter and coconut sugar (measured to desired sweetness, 1/2 c. yields a very mildly sweet cake) in the bowl of a standing mixer fitted with the paddle attachment. Mix on high speed until pale and fluffy, about 3-4 minutes. *[Note: If skipping the coconut sugar, beat butter until slightly fluffy, about 1-2 minutes.]*
3. Add eggs, bananas, coconut milk, and vanilla extract. Beat on medium speed until smooth. Add coconut flour, baking powder, baking soda, toasted caraway seeds, and sea salt. Beat until smooth. Pour batter into greased loaf pan and sprinkle with nigella seeds. Bake for 65-80 minutes, or until golden brown and a toothpick inserted into the center comes out clean.
4. Allow to cool minimum 30 minutes in the pan before inverting onto a cooling rack. Cool completely before serving.
5. Top with Lemon Cream Glaze (pg. 44) or Chocolate Hazelnut Sauce (pg. 66), as desired.

CHOCOLATEY CACAO CUPCAKES

Rich, cacao cupcakes packed with melty morsels of chocolate. Topped with a creamy buttercream made with no butter or powdered sugar (pictured on pg. 8)

Chocolate Cupcakes

3	pastured eggs
1 can	full fat coconut milk
1/4 c.	organic grade B maple syrup (or 1/2 c. Date Paste, pg. 40)
1 T.	vanilla extract
1/2 c.	raw cacao powder
3 T.	virgin coconut oil
3/4 C.	organic coconut flour
1 t.	baking powder
1/2 t.	baking soda
1/2 c.	Enjoy Life Mini Chocolate Chips

Cacao Cream Frosting

4 oz.	100% cacao liquor/paste, chopped
2/3 c.	organic coconut cream
2 T.	organic grade B maple syrup (optional)
1 t.	vanilla extract
1/2 c.	raw cacao powder
	raw cacao nibs, for topping

Yields: 12 cupcakes

Directions:

1. Preheat oven to 350F.
2. *Make the cakes*: In a small saucepan, combine cocoa powder and coconut oil. Cook until cocoa powder is melted. Set aside.
3. In the bowl of a stand mixer fitted with a paddle attachment, combine eggs, coconut milk, maple syrup, and vanilla extract. Mix on medium speed until well combined. With the mixer on low speed, slowly drizzle in the cocoa powder/coconut oil mixture and mix to combine. Add coconut flour, baking powder, baking soda, and mix on medium speed until batter is smooth, about 60 seconds. Add chocolate chips and mix on low speed to combine.
4. Portion batter evenly between 12 lined muffin cups. Bake for 45-60 minutes, or until a toothpick comes out clean.
5. *Make the frosting*: In the bowl of a stand mixer, combine cocoa liquor, maple syrup, vanilla extract, and coconut cream. Place the mixture over a bowl of simmering water on medium low heat. Mix frequently until mixture is warmed through and chocolate is melted. Place in the refrigerator to cool 1 hour.
6. Remove from fridge, add cocoa powder to the bowl, and place on the stand mixer. Mix on low to incorporate cocoa powder. Move to medium high speed and mix until it reaches a thick, frosting-like consistency. Pipe or spread onto cooled cupcakes. Sprinkle with cacao nibs and serve.

A moist chai-infused cake, packed with nutrients from fresh carrots. Beautifully dressed up for a special occasion or enjoy dressed down for a weekend treat.

Carrot Cake

1 can	can organic full-fat coconut milk
6	pastured eggs
1/3 c.	raw honey (or 2/3 c. Date Paste, pg. 40)
1/4 c.	virgin coconut oil
1 t.	vanilla extract
2 1/2 c.	blanched almond flour
1/3 c.	organic coconut flour
1 t.	sea salt
1 1/2 t.	baking powder
1/2 t.	baking soda
3 c.	shredded carrot pulp
12 oz.	fresh figs (about 12)

Chai Spices

2 t.	ground cinnamon
1 t.	ground ginger
1/8 t.	ground cloves
1/8 t.	ground nutmeg
1/8 t.	ground cardamom
pinch	black pepper, finely ground

Directions:

1. *Note on carrot pulp*: to get 3 cups of carrot pulp, juice 8 carrots in a cold-pressed juicer, set aside juice and reserve pulp. OR shred 8 carrots with a box shredder, place the shredded carrot in a tea towel, and squeeze tightly to press much of the juice out.

2. *Preheat oven to 350F.* In a small saucepan, combine 1 can coconut milk with chai spices. Bring to a simmer over medium heat, cover with a lid, and remove from heat. Let steep for 10-15 minutes.

3. *Make the cake:* combine eggs, honey, coconut oil, and vanilla extract in the bowl of a stand mixer. Mix on medium speed until well-combined. With the mixer on low, slowly pour in the warm coconut milk mixture. Increase speed to medium to mix well. Add in almond flour, coconut flour, salt, baking powder, baking soda, and carrot pulp and mix on high to combine. Divide batter equally between *two 9-inch greased pie pans*.

4. Bake for 45-50 minutes, or until toothpick comes out clean. Cool in pans 20 minutes before inverting onto a cooling rack. Cool completely before frosting.

5. *Make the frosting*: place coconut butter, maple syrup, cinnamon, and vanilla powder in the bowl of a stand mixer fitter with the whisk attachment. Whisk on medium speed for 1-2 minutes, or until coconut butter is smooth and volume increases by 50%. Add in Cultured Coconut "Cream Cheese" and whisk on high until fully incorporated. Frosting should resemble the texture of a smooth and thick buttercream. If frosting is too thick to spread, add coconut milk (1 teaspoon at a time) to thin out to desired texture.

6. Spread frosting onto cooled cakes, placing a thin layer between the two rounds. Top with fresh figs.

Maple Cream Frosting

1/2 c.	organic coconut butter
3 T.	organic grade B maple syrup (or 1/3 c. Date Paste, pg. 40)
1/2 t.	ground cinnamon
1 t.	vanilla powder
1 c.	Cultured Coconut "Cream Cheese" (pg. 11)

CHAI-SPICED CARROT CAKE WITH MAPLE CREAM FROSTING

S'mores Pie, pg. 23

PIES & TARTS

A quick and light dessert with a simple ingredient list. Pecans pair beautifully with sweet, tart fruit. If you don't have access to fresh strawberries, use whatever you have in season.

Pecan Crust

2 c.	raw pecans
5	dried medjool dates
3 T.	organic virgin coconut oil
1/2 t.	sea salt

Strawberry Filling

2 lbs.	fresh strawberries, sliced
1	lemon, juiced
1 t.	raw honey (optional)

Directions:

1. Make the crust: soak the pecans for 15 minutes in filtered water. Drain the water and place pecans, dates, coconut oil, and sea salt in the bowl of a large food processor. Process until a wet paste forms. Press a thin layer into a 14 x 4.5" (shown at right) or a 9" round tart pan. Refrigerate for 30 minutes before filling.
2. Make the filling: whisk the lemon juice and honey together until honey is dissolved. Add strawberries and toss to coat. Set aside for 15 minutes to let the strawberries macerate.
3. Fill the chilled pecan crust with the macerated strawberries. Top with Whipped Coconut Cream Topping and serve immediately. Tart can be stored covered and refrigerated but is best enjoyed fresh.

Whipped Coconut Cream Topping

2/3 c.	organic coconut cream

Directions:

1. Remove coconut cream from a refrigerated can of organic full-fat coconut milk (unless you've purchased 100% coconut cream, see Appendix pg. 69).
2. Scoop into the bowl of a stand mixer. Place the bowl in the freezer for 5 minutes.
3. Remove from the freezer and place on a stand mixer fitted with the whisk attachment. Whisk on high speed until coconut cream stiffens (about 60 seconds) and holds stiff peaks when scooped. Serve immediately.

COOL STRAWBERRY PECAN TART

BANANA CREAM PIE

Mini pies sized for a perfectly portioned treat. Mildly sweet pastry cream fills a graham-flavored crust, garnished with nutty, toasted banana and whipped coconut cream.

Yields: 8 mini-pies or 1 9-inch pie

Pastry Cream

5	pastured egg yolks
1 c.	organic full-fat coconut milk
1	lemon, juiced
1/4 c.	raw honey
1/4 c.	tapioca starch
1	vanilla bean (or 1 t. vanilla extract)
	pinch sea salt

Pastry Cream Directions:

Combine ingredients in a medium saucepan and place over medium low heat. Whisk frequently until filling thickens to a creamy consistency, about 5-10 minutes. Remove from heat.

Graham Crust

3 c.	blanched almond flour
2 T.	blackstrap molasses
1/4 c.	organic virgin coconut oil
1 t.	sea salt

Graham Crust Directions:

Preheat oven to 350F. Combine all ingredients in the bowl of a large food processor. Process until fully combined. Press into pie tin(s) and bake for 15 minutes, or until golden. Remove and let cool to room temperature.

To Assemble

2	bananas, divided
1 T.	organic virgin coconut oil

Directions to Assemble:

1. Slice one banana into 1/2" slices. Heat a non-stick skillet over medium heat. Add coconut oil and bananas and saute until golden brown, about 3 minutes per side. Move to a paper towel to cool.
2. Slice the second banana into very thin slices. Place the slices down in a single, even layer at the bottom of the baked graham crusts. Fill the pie(s) with pastry cream, portioning evenly. Chill pies 1+ hours before serving.
3. To serve: top with a dollop of Whipped Coconut Cream (pg. 20) and a slice of sautéed banana.

S'MORES PIE

Reminiscent of campfire fun, this pie is perfect for cool weather nights. Comes together in under an hour and should be enjoyed immediately for maximum marshmallow gooeyness (pictured on pg. 18).

Graham Crust

3 c.	blanched almond flour
2 T.	blackstrap molasses
1/4 c.	organic virgin coconut oil
1 t.	sea salt

Chocolate Custard Filling

5	pastured egg yolks
1 c.	organic full-fat coconut milk
1/4 c.	organic grade B maple syrup
3/4 c.	raw cocoa powder
1/4 c.	tapioca starch
1/4 t.	instant espresso powder
1 T.	vanilla extract
	pinch sea salt

Maple Marshmallow Topping

1/2 c.	raw honey
1/2 c.	organic grade B maple syrup
	pinch sea salt
2 T.	grass-fed gelatin
1/2 c.	filtered water
1 t.	vanilla extract

Directions:

1. *Make the crust*: preheat oven to 350F. Combine all ingredients in the bowl of a food processor. Process until fully combined and crumbly. Press into 9-inch tart/pie pan and bake for 12-15 minutes, or until golden. Remove and let cool 10 minutes before filling.

2. *While crust is cooling, prepare filling.* Combine all ingredients in a medium saucepan and place over medium low heat. Whisk frequently until filling thickens to a creamy consistency, about 5-10 minutes (the longer it's cooked, the thicker it will get). Remove from heat and pour into cooled Graham Crust. Move pie to the fridge to cool and set custard, about 20-30 minutes.

3. *While the filling is setting, prepare the topping.* Mix honey, maple syrup, and salt in a small saucepan over medium heat. Bring to a simmer and cook until reduced by half and darker in color, about 5-10 minutes (about 280F on a candy thermometer).

4. While the syrup is cooking, place filtered water in the bowl of a stand mixer. Sprinkle gelatin over the water to dissolve. With the mixer running on low, drizzle hot maple syrup mixture in the side of the bowl slowly. Move the speed to medium for 1-2 minutes. Move the speed to high for 3-5 more minutes, or until doubled in volume. Add vanilla extract and whip on high for another 1-2 minutes, or until mixture is fully cooled.

5. Scoop marshmallow onto the cooled pie, spreading evenly and creating some fun peaks as you spread. Torch with a handheld blowtorch (every kitchen should have one!) or place under the broiler: low setting, with the oven rack positioned at the bottom for 1-2 minutes, or until browned. Watch carefully because it will burn quickly. Serve immediately!

APPLE & SAGE HAND PIES

Full fall flavor in a personal-sized pie. Light, flaky, and filled with warm sage-scented apples. Let them cool before enjoying to ensure a crisp, buttery crust.

Almond Flax Pastry Dough

3 c.	blanched almond flour
3/4 c.	tapioca starch
1/2 c.	ground flaxseed
1	pastured egg
1/2 c.	grass-fed butter, cold and cubed to 1"
2 T.	raw honey
1 t.	sea salt

Apple Sage Filling

1/4 c.	grass-fed butter or virgin coconut oil
4	organic apples, very finely diced
1/2 t.	sea salt
4	medium fresh sage leaves, chopped
1-2 T.	organic grade B maple syrup
1 t.	vanilla extract
1	pastured egg + 1 t. filtered water, for glazing

Directions:

1. *Prepare the crust*: combine all ingredients in the bowl of a large food processor and process to combine, about 60-90 seconds. Dough should come together in clumps and hold together when pinched between two fingers. Dump dough onto a large piece of saran wrap, wrap tightly, and place in the refrigerator for 30-60 minutes to chill.

2. While dough is chilling, *prepare filling*. Melt butter in a large skillet over medium-low heat. Continue to cook (butter will bubble) until butter begins to brown. Promptly add diced apple pieces and sea salt and stir well. Turn heat to medium and cook until apples are softened, about 10 minutes. Add sage, maple syrup, and vanilla. Stir well (vanilla will cause mixture to bubble) and cook to reduce the syrup, about 2-3 minutes.

3. *Assemble the pies*: preheat oven to 400F. Remove dough from fridge. Place half the chilled dough between two large pieces of parchment and roll with rolling pin to 1/2" thickness. Try to handle the dough as little as possible, as not to warm it too much. Lift the top layer of parchment and cut 8 4" rounds with a cookie cutter or large rimmed glass. Place the rounds on a parchment lined sheet pan.

4. Equally distribute the filling between the 8 rounds, about 2 T. each. Roll out the remaining dough and cut 8 more rounds. Lay one of each on the rounds already laid out with the filling and press the edges down with the blade of a fork.

5. Whisk together egg and water in a small bowl and using a pastry brush, lightly glaze the tops of each pie. Immediately bake for 13-15 minutes, or until golden brown. Move to a cooling rack and cool for 10-15 minutes before enjoying (pies will crumble if they are not left to cool before eating).

CARAMELIZED COCONUT FLAN

> A Mexican staple made wholesome with coconut milk. A layer of caramelized honey yields a light sauce with a nutty flavor.

Flan

1/2 c.	raw honey
2 T.	filtered water
1	lemon, juiced
1/2 c.	Sweetened Condensed Coconut Milk
1 can	organic full-fat coconut milk
1	vanilla bean, split and seeds scraped
1	cinnamon stick
1/4 t.	sea salt
3	pastured eggs
2	pastured egg yolks

Sweetened Condensed Coconut Milk

1 can	organic full-fat coconut milk
1/4 c.	raw honey

Directions:

1. Preheat oven to 325F. Have ready a 2-quart nonstick flan mold and a large roasting pan.
2. In a small saucepan, combine raw honey and filtered water. Cook over medium heat until mixture reduces and turns a dark caramel color, about 280F (warning: it will burn at 300F+). Remove from heat and stir in lemon juice (mixture will bubble a bit) and pour into flan mold. Tilt the mold to swirl the caramelized honey around the sides. Place the mold into the roasting pan and set aside.
3. *Prepare the Sweetened Condensed Coconut Milk* by combining 1 can coconut milk and ¼ c. raw honey in a medium saucepan. Cook over medium heat, stirring occasionally, until mixture turns slightly caramel in color and reduces to ½ cup total volume, about 20-30 minutes.
4. To the completed Sweetened Condensed Coconut Milk, add 1 can coconut milk, vanilla bean (seeds AND bean), cinnamon stick, and sea salt. Whisk well and bring to a simmer. Remove from heat, cover with a lid, and let steep 10 minutes.
5. In a separate bowl, whisk together eggs and egg yolks. Add a small amount of the warm coconut milk to the eggs and whisk quickly to prevent the eggs from cooking. Add the remaining coconut mixture to the bowl, whisking constantly. Pour the entire mixture through a strainer set over a large measuring cup (4-cup minimum), discard the bits in the strainer, and pour the coconut/egg mixture into the flan mold.
6. Create a water bath by filling the roasting pan halfway with warm water, careful not to get any water in the flan mold. Carefully place in the oven and cook 50 minutes to 1 hour, or until center is set and jiggles slightly. Remove from oven and cool the flan completely in the water bath. Transfer flan to the refrigerator and chill a minimum of 4 hours before serving.
7. To serve, run a knife around the edge of the mold to loosen the flan. Place a serving plate over the mold and invert to remove flan. Serve chilled as-is or top with Whipped Coconut Cream (pg. 20), as desired.

Almond Flax Crust

3 c.	almond flour
3/4 c.	tapioca starch
1/2 c.	ground flaxseed
1	pastured egg
1/2 c.	grass-fed butter, cold and cubed to 1"
2 T.	raw honey (or 2 T. Date Paste, pg. 40)
1 t.	sea salt
1	pastured egg + 1 t. filtered water

Blueberry Filling

3 c.	fresh blueberries
1/2	lemon, juiced
1 T.	tapioca starch

Directions:

1. Preheat oven to 350F. Mix blueberries, lemon juice, and tapioca starch in a large bowl. Set aside.

2. Cut 2 sheets of parchment to the size of your baking sheet. Between the 2 sheets, roll out pastry dough to ½" thickness, creating an oblong circle. Move the sheets and dough carefully to your baking sheet and remove the top piece of parchment.

3. Dump the blueberry mix onto the middle of the pastry dough, leaving a 2" border of dough. Moving gently around the circle, lift the crust onto the blueberries, overlapping and securing as you go. Once the entire edge is pressed against the blueberries, smooth cracks in the dough with your fingers, paying attention to the bottom edge (area closest to the pan) of the pie.

4. Whisk together 1 egg with 1 t. water. Using a pastry brush, coat the entire surface of the dough.

5. Bake for 30-35 minutes or until golden brown. Remove from oven and let cool minimum of 30 minutes before serving (this will keep the pie from crumbling when cutting into it). Serve as-is or top with Whipped Coconut Cream Topping (pg. 20).

A free-form pie filled with warm, juicy blueberries. Allowing the galette to cool for 30 minutes after cooking will ensure a moist, buttery crust.

Maple
Bacon
Caramel
Apples
pg. 36

CANDY & CHOCOLATE

Chocolate Layers

8 oz.	100% cacao liquor/paste, chopped
1/4 c.	organic grade B maple syrup
1/2 c.	raw almond butter

Caramel

1/2 c.	organic grade B maple syrup
1/3 c.	organic coconut cream
1/2 t.	sea salt
1 T.	vanilla extract
1 T.	grass-fed butter or virgin coconut oil

Nougat

2 T.	grass-fed butter or virgin coconut oil
2 T.	organic grade B maple syrup
2 T.	organic coconut cream
1/4 c.	raw almond butter
1 c.	roasted almonds, roughly chopped
1 t.	vanilla extract
2 t.	grass-fed gelatin
3/4 c.	filtered water, divided
1/2 c.	organic grade B maple syrup

Directions:

1. Cut two pieces of parchment or wax paper to 8" by 12." Line an 8x8x2" pan with the sheets facing opposite directions and press into corners. Paper should come up the sides to act as 'handles' when lifting the finished "ShNickers" out.

2. *Make the chocolate layers*: in a bowl placed over a pot of low simmering water (double boiler), combine chopped cacao paste, maple syrup, and almond butter. Whisk until chocolate is melted and mixture is smooth. Pour half the mixture into the parchment lined baking pan and set the other half aside for later. Freeze for 5-10 minutes or until chocolate is solid.

3. *Make the caramel layer*: maple syrup, coconut cream, and sea salt in a shallow saucepan over medium heat. Whisk together and bring to a boil, cooking until the mixture reaches 300F, about 30 minutes (it should become thick and caramel-like in texture). Remove from heat and whisk in vanilla extract and butter. Pour over chilled chocolate layer, smooth out, and place back in the freezer for 10-15 minutes.

4. *Make the nougat layer*: combine butter, 2 T. maple syrup, and coconut cream in a saucepan over medium heat. Bring to a boil and cook 3-5 minutes, or until mixture reduces by ½. Add in almond butter, chopped almonds, and vanilla extract. Stir until mixture is smooth and set aside.

5. Pour ¼ c. water into the bowl of stand mixer fitted with the whisk attachment. Sprinkle gelatin over water to dissolve. In a separate small saucepan, combine ½ c. maple syrup and ½ c. water. Bring to a boil and cook until mixture reduces by half and reaches 280F. With the mixer running on low speed, drizzle in the reduced maple syrup mixture. Move speed to medium for 60 seconds, then to high for 2-3 minutes or until mixture doubles in volume and resembles a creamy marshmallow texture.

6. Add the reserved almond butter/nut mixture into the maple marshmallow and mix well. Pour mixture onto the chilled caramel and smooth it out. Top with remaining ½ chocolate layer and place back in the freezer. Freeze minimum 1 hour before serving. Best enjoyed chilled or frozen.

"ShNICKERS"

Yields: 1 8x8" pan

A whole foods approach to a classic American candy bar. Chewy, gooey, and chocolatey--these bars are addictive! This recipe can be doubled (or tripled!) and frozen for months.

DARK CITRUS PUNCH
TRUFFLES

A simple recipe for a rich treat that packs quite a citrus flavor 'punch.' Can be made without maple syrup for a 100% dark truffle. Vegan and soy-free.

Yields: approx. 20 2" truffles

10 oz.	100% cacao paste/liquor, chopped	1/2	small orange, juiced
3 T.	organic grade B maple syrup	1	lemon, zest
2 t.	vanilla extract	1	orange, zest
1/4 c.	organic virgin coconut oil		pinch sea salt
1/2	lemon, juiced	1/2 c.	raw cacao powder, for rolling

Directions:

1. Mix chopped cacao, maple syrup, and vanilla extract in a bowl and set aside.

2. Combine coconut oil, lemon juice, orange juice, zest, and sea salt in a small saucepan over medium-low heat. Bring to a simmer, cover, and cook 5 minutes on low heat. Remove from heat and leave covered 10 minutes to steep.

3. Strain coconut oil/citrus mixture through a fine strainer, discard the zest, and pour over chocolate. Cover with plastic wrap for 5 minutes to warm the chocolate through. Remove plastic wrap and stir well until all the chocolate is melted.

4. Cover again and place the bowl in the refrigerator to set the chocolate. Once chilled, remove and bring to room temperature before using a #60 disher to scoop truffles to your size preference. Roll each truffle in cacao powder (coat well) and allow to set briefly. Enjoy immediately! Truffles are best stored between 60- 70F but not refrigerated.

MAPLE BACON CARAMEL APPLES

A little bacon grease gives this caramel a smoky, salty edge. Chill the apples immediately after dipping to prevent the toppings from running off (pictured on pg. 30).

Yields: 4 caramel apples

1/2 c.	organic coconut cream	4	medium organic apples, washed
1 c.	organic grade B maple syrup	4	thick-sliced grass-fed bacon, cooked crisp
1/2 t.	sea salt	1/2 c.	roasted almonds, chopped fine
2 t.	vanilla extract	4	skewers
1 T.	bacon grease		

Directions:

1. Combine coconut cream, maple syrup, and sea salt in a wide-bottom saucepan. Bring to a simmer over medium heat and cook until caramel has reduced by half and reaches 300F. Remove from heat and whisk in vanilla extract and reserved bacon grease.
2. Have a parchment lined plate ready. Remove any stems from the apples and place a skewer down the center from the top.
3. Pour the hot caramel into a deep cup, wide enough for dipping the apples. Break up bacon into small pieces and mix with the chopped almonds in a wide, shallow dish. Dip each apple into the caramel, allowing excess caramel to drip off. Roll the dipped apple in the bacon/almond mix. Set onto the parchment. Working quickly, continue with the remaining apples.
4. Place the plate in a freezer to set the caramel (this will help to keep the caramel from running off the apples) for 30 minutes. Remove and serve. Store in the refrigerator for up to a week.

Crispies

2 c.	pepitas
1 c.	sliced almonds
1 c.	large unsweetened coconut flakes

Marshmallow Cream

1/4 c.	raw honey
1/4 c.	organic coconut sugar
1/2 t.	sea salt
1/4 c.	filtered water
1 T.	grass-fed gelatin
1 T.	coconut or vanilla extract
1 c.	unsweetened coconut flakes
1 T.	organic virgin coconut oil, for greasing

TOASTED COCONUT CRISPY TREATS

Directions:

1. *Prepare the crispies*: preheat oven to 350F. Place pepitas and sliced almonds on a dry half sheet pan. Cook for 10 minutes. Remove pan, toss in coconut flakes, and cook for another 5-10 minutes, or until coconut begins to brown. Remove from oven, transfer to a bowl and allow to cool. Place separate 1 cup of coconut flakes on the sheet pan and cook for 5-10 minutes or until lightly browned. Set aside in a separate bowl for garnishing later.

2. While the crispies are roasting, *prepare marshmallow cream*. Place honey, coconut sugar, and salt in a small saucepan. Cook over medium heat until mixture reaches 240F on a candy thermometer.

3. While mixture is cooking, place water and gelatin in the bowl of a stand mixer fitted with a whisk attachment. Sprinkle gelatin over the water to dissolve.

4. Once honey mixture reaches 240F, turn on mixer to low speed and drizzle the hot mixture into the side of the stand mixer bowl, careful not to splash it. Once all of the hot mixture is mixed into the gelatin, turn the mixer up to medium speed for 1-2 minutes. Then move the speed to high and mix another 1-2 minutes, or until the mixture is fluffy and has doubled in volume. Add the coconut extract and whip 30 seconds to combine.

5. Remove the bowl from the stand mixer and mix in the dry crispies, stirring well. Pour the mixture into an 8x8" pan that's been greased with coconut oil. Press the mixture evenly into the pan and sprinkle with reserved toasted coconut flakes.

6. Allow to set for 4+ hours before slicing and serving. You can serve before this, but they will be a bit gooey!

MACA
SUPER BARK

6 oz.	100% cacao paste/liquor, chopped & divided
2-4 T.	organic grade B maple syrup (optional)
1 t.	organic virgin coconut oil
1 T.	raw maca powder
1 c.	dried fruit of choice, chopped
1/2 c.	sliced almonds, toasted
1 T.	chia seeds
	grey sea salt or fleur de sel, to taste

Directions:

1. Have ready a quarter-sheet pan lined with parchment paper or a silpat mat.

2. Combine 2/3 of the chopped cacao paste with the maple syrup (adjust to taste), and coconut oil in a heat-proof bowl. Place the bowl over a saucepan of simmering water on low heat. Stir until the mixture comes to 115F on a candy thermometer (it should feel warm to the touch but not hot).

3. Remove the bowl from heat and in the remaining 1/3 chopped cacao. Stir until melted. Pour onto parchment lined sheet pan and spread thin with an offset spatula. Top with dried fruit, almonds, chia, and sea salt.

4. Move the sheet pan to the freezer for 15 minutes to harden. Remove from the freezer and let come to room temperature (70-74F) before enjoying. Best stored below 70F but not refrigerated.

Flavorful chocolate bark that's packed with a diverse array of nutrients. Maca is rich in vitamins and naturally gives a little energy boost. Follow the directions closely for perfectly tempered chocolate with snap and shine.

Drinking Chocolate

1 can	organic full-fat coconut milk
1 c.	filtered water
1-2 t.	1-2 t. organic lavender buds (adjust to taste)
4 oz.	100% cacao paste/liquor, chopped
1-2 T.	raw honey (or 1/4 c. Date Paste, see below)
1 T.	raw cacao powder
1 t.	vanilla extract
	pinch sea salt

Drinking Chocolate Directions:

1. Combine coconut milk, water, and lavender in a small saucepan over medium heat. Bring to a simmer, cover, and cook 5 minutes.
2. Remove from heat and leave covered 10 minutes to let steep.
3. Strain mixture through a fine strainer and pour liquid back into the saucepan. Add in chopped cacao paste, honey, cacao powder, vanilla extract, and sea salt. Cook over medium heat until chocolate is melted, whisking occasionally.
4. Remove from heat and serve immediately. Top with Whipped Coconut Cream (pg. 20), as desired.

Date Paste

15	dried medjool dates, pitted
3/4 c.	warm filtered water

Date Paste Directions:

1. Combine the dates and filtered water in a high-powered blender. Cover and let soak 10 minutes. Blend on high for 1-2 minutes, or until mixture becomes a thick, smooth paste.

LAVENDER
DARK
DRINKING
CHOCOLATE

Coconut Caramel Cookies, pg. 48

COOKIES & BARS

Creamy, flaky bars packed with bright lemon flavor. These bars are great served warm, at room temperature, or even chilled. Yields: 9 bars

Crust

1 1/2 c.	blanched almond flour
6 T.	tapioca starch
1 t.	lemon, zest (reserve juice for glaze)
1/4 t.	sea salt
1/4 c.	grass fed butter, cold and cubed to 1"
1 T.	raw honey

Lemon Filling

3	pastured eggs
1/3 c.	raw honey
1	lemon, juice & zest
1 t.	vanilla extract
1/2 c.	blanched almond flour
1 T.	tapioca starch
1/4 t.	sea salt

Lemon Cream Glaze

1 T.	raw honey	1	lemon, juiced
2 T.	grass-fed butter or virgin coconut oil	1/4 c.	organic coconut butter

Directions:

1. Preheat oven to 325F.

2. *Make the crust*: combine almond flour, tapioca starch, lemon zest, and sea salt in the bowl of a food processor. Pulse to combine. Add cold butter cubes and raw honey and pulse again (lightly) until crust just barely comes together. It will be crumbly. Press into an 8x8" baking pan. Bake for 20 minutes, or until golden. Remove and let cool.

3. Leave oven heated at 325F.

4. *Make the filling*: combine eggs, honey, lemon juice and zest, and vanilla extract in the same food processor bowl previously used for the crust. Process until combined and pale yellow, about 60 seconds. Add almond flour, tapioca starch, and sea salt. Process again to combine, about 30 seconds. Scrape down sides and process another 30 seconds. Pour into cooled crust and bake 25-30 minutes, or until center is set.

5. *Make the glaze*: combine ingredients in a small saucepan over medium-low heat. Cook until everything is melted and smooth, whisking frequently. Remove from heat and pour onto cooked filling. To set the glaze (if desired), refrigerate 30 minutes before serving. Best stored at room temperature in a sealed container.

CREAMY LEMON BARS

Moist, chewy brownies with a little kick of heat. Make your own cultured coconut "cream cheese" for a tangy frosting or substitute with regular coconut cream for a frosting with a little less zing.

MEXICAN

HOT

CHOCOLATE BROWNIES

Yields: 9 brownies

Brownies

1/4 c.	filtered water
2 oz.	100% cacao paste/liquor, plus more for garnish
3 T.	organic grade B maple syrup (or 1/3 c. Date Paste, pg. 40)
3 T.	blackstrap molasses
1/4 c.	avocado oil
2 T.	virgin coconut oil, plus more for greasing
1/4 c.	raw cacao powder
1/2 t.	instant espresso powder
2	pastured eggs
2	pastured egg yolks
1 t.	vanilla extract
2 T.	ground cinnamon
1/2 t.	ground cayenne pepper
1/2 t.	sea salt
1/3 c.	organic coconut flour
1/4 c.	mini chocolate chips (or chopped 100% cacao for less sweetness)

Directions:

1. Preheat oven to 350F.

2. *Make the brownies*: combine water, cacao paste, maple syrup, molasses, avocado oil, coconut oil, cacao powder, and instant espresso in a medium saucepan. Cook over medium heat and whisk until smooth.

3. In the bowl of a stand mixer, add eggs, egg yolks, vanilla extract, cinnamon, cayenne pepper, and sea salt and mix on high to combine. With the mixer on low, slowly drizzle in warm chocolate mixture. Move to medium speed for 1-2 minutes until smooth, scraping down the sides halfway through.

4. Add coconut flour and beat another 30-60 seconds, or until smooth. Remove the bowl and fold in the chocolate chips.

5. Pour into a greased 8x8 baking pan and bake for 25-30 minutes, or until a toothpick comes out clean. Cool completely before frosting.

6. *Make the frosting*: in a clean bowl of a stand mixer fitted with the whisk attachment, combine coconut butter, honey, and vanilla powder. Mix on medium speed until smooth and fluffy. Add in "cream cheese" and beat on high 60 seconds. Frost cooled brownies and garnish with shaved 100% cacao, as desired.

Note: if making this with Date Paste for a sugar-free dessert, leave out blackstrap molasses

"Cream Cheese" Frosting

1/4 c.	organic coconut butter
2-4 T.	raw honey (or 1/4 c. Date Paste, pg. 40)
1 t.	vanilla powder
1/2 c.	Cultured Coconut "Cream Cheese" (pg. 9)

Cookies

2 c.	blanched almond flour
1 T.	tapioca starch
1/4 c.	ground flaxseed
4 T.	organic virgin coconut oil
1 T.	raw honey
1/2 t.	sea salt

Honey Caramel

1/2 c.	raw honey
1/3 c.	organic coconut cream
1/2 t.	sea salt
1 T.	vanilla extract
1 T.	grass-fed butter or virgin coconut oil

Coconut Topping

1 1/2 c.	shredded unsweetened coconut
1/2 c.	Honey Caramel (recipe on right)

Chocolate Drizzle

2 oz.	100% cocoa paste/liquor, chopped
2 T.	organic grade B maple syrup
2 T.	organic virgin coconut oil

Directions:

1. *Make the cookie dough*: combine all ingredients in the bowl of a food processor. Process until fully combined and dough holds together when pinched. Dump out onto plastic wrap, wrap tightly, and refrigerate for 30+ minutes.

2. *Make the caramel*: combine honey, coconut cream, and sea salt in a medium saucepan. Whisk well and bring to a simmer over medium heat. Continue to heat until mixture reduces by 1/3 and turns a caramel color (if using a candy thermometer, the caramel will read approximately 300F). Remove from heat and add vanilla extract and butter, whisk well, and set aside to cool.

3. *Cut and cook the cookies*: preheat oven to 325F. Remove dough from refrigerator. Place half the dough in between 2 sheets of parchment paper and roll carefully to 1/4" thickness. Remove the top sheet of parchment and cut cookie shapes. A 3" fluted round cutter and with a 1" fluted to cut out the center hole were used here. (The center hole does not need to be cut, it's purely for decoration!) Gather scraps and combine with remaining dough and repeat the rolling & cutting. Continue until all the dough is used, yielding about 12 cookies.

4. Arrange on a parchment-lined baking sheet and bake for 9-10 minutes, or until slightly golden. Remove from oven, move cookies to a cooling rack and cool completely before topping.

5. *Make the topping*: spread 1½ c. shredded unsweetened coconut onto a sheet pan. Cook at 325F for 10 minutes, tossing frequently to ensure even browning (it will burn easily so keep a close eye on it!). Remove and let cool.

6. Spread a thin layer of caramel on each cookie (this gives the topping something to stick to). Mix the toasted coconut flakes with ½ c. caramel. Using your fingers, press topping onto each cookie to ½" thickness (as shown in the bottom left picture to the right). Move cookies to the refrigerator for 10 minutes to set.

7. *Make the chocolate drizzle & assemble*: mix all chocolate drizzle ingredients in a small saucepan over medium-low heat, stirring frequently. Once chocolate is melted, remove from heat. Remove cookies from refrigerator and carefully dip just the bottom of the cookies into the melted chocolate (creating an even layer of chocolate on the bottom of each cookie) and place them back onto parchment. Use a fork to flick chocolate across the tops, as desired. Place back into the refrigerator for 10-15 minutes to set chocolate before eating. Cookies will keep best if stored at room temperature in layers of parchment.

A grain-free version of an old-timey American favorite made famous by girl scouts. Crisp, chewy, and very satisfying. <u>Yields:</u> 12 cookies

COCONUT CARAMEL COOKIES

BLACKBERRY CRUMBLE BARS

Crumbly bars bursting with moist, blackberry flavor. The amount of honey listed will yield a very mildly sweet (and extra tart!) bar but can be adjusted to personal taste.

Blackberry Filling

18 oz.	fresh blackberries, divided
1	lemon, juiced
1 t.	raw honey, warmed
1/2 t.	vanilla extract
	pinch sea salt

Crust & Crumble

3 c.	blanched almond flour
3/4 c.	tapioca starch
1	lemon, zest
1/2 t.	sea salt
pinch	ground cinnamon
6 T.	grass-fed butter, cold and cubed to 1"
3 T.	raw honey
1	pastured egg
1/2 c.	raw sliced slmonds

Yields: 9 bars

Directions:

1. Preheat oven to 325F.
2. *Make the filling*: combine 12 oz blackberries with lemon juice, honey, vanilla extract, and sea salt. Mash blackberries with a fork (watch for splatters!) and mix well. Add remaining 6 oz blackberries (do not mash), stir to combine, and set aside.
3. *Make the crust & crumble*: combine almond flour, tapioca starch, lemon zest, sea salt, and ground cinnamon in the bowl of a large food processor. Pulse to combine. Add butter, honey, and egg. Pulse again to combine. Dough will be crumbly; do not over-mix.
4. *Assemble*: move 2/3 of the dough to an 8x8" baking pan. Press into an even layer. Top with blackberry filling.
5. Add ½ c. sliced almonds to the remaining 1/3 dough remaining in the food processor. Pulse briefly to incorporate. Crumble over the blackberry filling in large chunks. Do not press in. Bake for 30-35 minutes, or until golden brown.

> *A fun-shaped, spicy cookie that's perfect for the fall and winter months. Dried fruits give these soft cookies extra flavor and a little chew.*

Cranberry Ginger Cookies

2 c.	blanched almond flour	2 T.	blackstrap molasses
1/4 c.	tapioca starch	2 T.	organic grade B maple syrup
1/4 c.	ground flaxseed	1 t.	vanilla extract
1/2 t.	sea salt	2 T.	organic virgin coconut oil
1 T.	ground cinnamon	1/4 c.	dried cranberries, chopped
1 t.	ground ginger	1/4 c.	crystallized ginger, chopped

Directions:

1. Preheat oven to 325F.
2. *Make the cookies*: combine almond flour, tapioca starch, flaxseed, sea salt, cinnamon, and ginger in the bowl of a large food processor. Pulse to combine. Add molasses, maple syrup, vanilla extract, coconut oil, cranberries, and ginger. Process until dough comes together in a large ball, about 30-60 seconds. Dump out onto a large piece of saran wrap, wrap tightly, and refrigerate 30+ minutes.

Maple Icing

1/4 c.	organic coconut butter
1/2 c.	organic coconut cream
4 T.	organic grade B maple syrup
1 t.	vanilla extract
	pinch ground cloves
2-4 T.	grass-fed butter, melted

3. Remove dough from the refrigerator. Place half the dough in between 2 sheets of parchment paper and roll carefully to 1/4" thickness. Remove the top sheet of parchment and cut cookie shapes. Gather scraps and combine with remaining dough and repeat the rolling & cutting. Continue until all the dough is used, yielding about 16 cookies. Divide the cut cookies between 2 parchment-lined sheet pans and bake 12-15 minutes each pan. Move cookies to a cooling rack and cool completely before frosting.
4. *Make the icing*: Combine all icing ingredients in the bowl of a stand mixer fitted with the paddle attachment. Beat on medium high speed until smooth and creamy. The amount of butter added will yield either a thicker icing for piping decorations (less butter) or a thinner icing for spreading evenly onto cookies (more butter).

Note: This icing recipe will yield enough to fully cover all 16 cookies; it can be halved if only used for piping decorations.

CRANBERRY GINGER COOKIES

Rich, chocolatey cookies reminiscent of the familiar chocolate sandwich cookie. The light and fluffy mint buttercream can be made with or without butter.

MINT CHOCOLATE SANDWICH COOKIES

Chocolate Cookies

2 c.	blanched almond flour
2/3 c.	2/3 c. raw cacao powder
2 T.	tapioca starch
1/4 c.	ground flaxseed
1/4 t.	instant espresso powder
2 T.	organic grade B maple syrup
1 t.	vanilla extract
1/2 t.	sea salt

Mint Buttercream

2	pastured egg whites
1/4 c.	raw honey
1/2 t.	sea salt
1 t.	mint extract
1/2 t.	vanilla extract
12 T.	grass-fed butter, softened (1 1/2 sticks)

Yields: 8 sandwich cookies

Directions:

1. *Prepare the cookies* by placing all ingredients into the bowl of a food processor. Process until ingredients are combined and dough comes into a ball and is slightly sticky. Dump dough onto a large piece of saran wrap, wrap tightly, and refrigerate for 30+ minutes.

2. Preheat oven to 325F. Once dough is chilled, place half between two sheets of parchment paper. Roll out to ¼" and cut with a 3" round cookie cutter. (Use a smaller cutter to get more cookies out of the batch.) Combine scraps with remaining dough and cut circles until all dough is used, totaling approximately 16 cookies.

3. Divide dough circles onto 2 parchment-lined baking sheets. Bake for 10 minutes per sheet. Move cookies to a cooling rack and cool completely before frosting.

4. *To prepare the buttercream*, whisk together egg whites, honey, and salt in the bowl of a stand mixer. Place the bowl over a separate small bowl of simmering water. Continue whisking until honey is melted and eggs are heated through. Move bowl back to stand mixer fitted with a whisk attachment. Mix on medium speed 60 seconds until eggs are frothy, move to high speed for 1-2 minutes until mixture has doubled in volume. Eggs should hold a stiff peak. Mix in mint and vanilla extracts and mix another 30 seconds.

5. With the mixer on high speed, slowly add the softened butter 1 tablespoon at a time. Mixture will look runny and slightly curdled at first but continue mixing on high speed 6-10 minutes (be patient), or until mixture becomes smooth and thick (like buttercream!). There should be no moisture visible when finished.

6. Spread or pipe buttercream over 8 cookies and sandwich with remaining 8 cookies. Eat immediately or let sit to soften 1-2 hours before eating. Cookies can be stored at room temperature but are best enjoyed fresh.

Notes:

-To make the buttercream without butter, simply stop after adding the extracts. Spread between cookies and enjoy immediately. Store in the fridge.

-Try different flavors by substituting the mint extract with any of your favorites, like almond or lemon.

Browned-Butter
Pumpkin Ice Cream
with Spicy Candied
Pecans, pg. 68

THE OTHER STUFF

One of my all-time favorite desserts. This version is both grain-free and dairy-free, yet still just as satisfying. Yields: 24 cream puffs

Bavarian Cream

2	pastured egg yolks
1/3 c.	organic full-fat coconut milk
1/2	lemon, juiced
2 T.	raw honey (or 1/4 c. Date Paste, pg. 40)
2 T.	tapioca starch
1 t.	vanilla extract
	pinch sea salt
1 1/2 c.	Whipped Coconut Cream, chilled (pg. 20)

Cream Puff

1/2 c.	filtered water
1 T.	organic virgin coconut oil
1/2 t.	sea salt
1/4 c.	tapioca starch
1/4 c.	potato starch
2	pastured eggs

Chocolate Glaze

4 oz.	100% cacao paste/liquor, chopped
2 T.	organic virgin coconut oil
2 t.	organic grade B maple syrup (optional)

Directions:

1. *Make the cream*: combine egg yolks, coconut milk, lemon juice, honey, tapioca starch, vanilla and sea salt in a large saucepan. Heat over medium heat, whisking frequently until mixture thickens, about 5-10 minutes. Move to refrigerator until cool, about 1 hour.

2. Add chilled Whipped Coconut Cream to the chilled cream by gently folding the two together, careful not to deflate the mixture too much. Scoop the cream into a large zip-top bag, twist tight and refrigerate until filling cream puffs, minimum 15 minutes.

3. *Make the cream puffs*: preheat oven to 450F. Have ready a half sheet pan lined with parchment. Combine the water, butter, and salt in a saucepan. Cook over medium heat until butter is melted. Add arrowroot and potato starch, mix quickly. The mixture will tighten, pull away from the sides, and get difficult to mix. Dump dough into the bowl of a stand mixer fitted with the paddle attachment. Mix on high until cooled, about 2 minutes. Move the speed to medium and add the eggs, one at a time. Move the speed back to high and mix until dough becomes smooth and pale yellow. It will be sticky and a little runny.

4. Scoop dough into a zip-top bag, twist tight and snip a small bit off the tip of the bag, about ¼." Pipe 12 2" circles onto the pan. Cook for 10 minutes at 450F. Lower temperature to 350F and cook for 20 more minutes. **Do not open the oven while the puffs are cooking.** Remove from the oven and move puffs to a cooling rack. Move the oven temperature back to 450F and repeat with the remaining 12 puffs. Cool puffs completely before filling.

5. *Make the glaze*: mix all chocolate glaze ingredients in a small saucepan over medium-low heat, stirring frequently. Once chocolate is melted, remove from heat. Set aside.

6. *Assemble the puffs*: using a sharp knife, cut the puffs in half. Remove the Bavarian Cream from the refrigerator and snip a bit off the tip, about ½." Fill each puff with cream and cap, as shown in the picture. Drizzle with Chocolate Glaze. Enjoy immediately or let sit for a bit for a softened puff. Best stored in the refrigerator.

BAVARIAN CREAM PUFFS

ALMOND PANNA COTTA
with raspberry & rhubarb jam

A creamy egg-free, dairy-free custard. For best results, use homemade almond milk but any milk of choice can be used here. <u>Yields: 4 servings</u>

Almond Panna Cotta

2 c.	homemade almond milk
6 T.	organic virgin coconut oil
1/4 c.	raw honey (or 1/2 c. Date Paste, pg. 40)
1 T.	almond extract
2 t.	vanilla extract
1 T.	grass-fed gelatin
1/2 t.	sea salt

Raspberry Rhubarb Jam

6 oz.	raspberries
6 oz.	rhubarb, diced small (fresh or frozen)
1	lemon, juiced
1/4 c.	raw honey (or 1/2 c. Date Paste, pg. 40)
1/8 t.	sea salt

Directions:

1. *Make the panna cotta*: combine all ingredients in a medium saucepan over medium heat. Whisk frequently until mixture starts to simmer. Remove from heat and portion into 4 glass jars or large ramekins. Move to the refrigerator and chill 1 hour.
2. *Make the jam*: combine all ingredients in a medium saucepan over medium heat. Stir well. Cover and bring to a boil, about 5-10 minutes. Remove the lid and cook uncovered until rhubarb breaks down and jam is fairly smooth (stirring occasionally), about 15-20 minutes. Remove from heat and let cool.
3. *To serve*: spoon jam on top of chilled panna cotta and enjoy.

A super-charged chocolate pop with a creamy crunch. The bitterness from the cacao nibs balances well with the richness of chocolate ice cream.

Bavarian Cream

1 can	organic full-fat coconut milk
1 t.	vanilla extract
1 T.	blackstrap molasses
3 T.	raw honey or 1/3 c. Date Paste, pg. 40 (both are optional)
1/4 c.	raw cacao powder
	pinch sea salt

Chocolate Dip

4 oz.	100% cacao paste/liquor, chopped
4 T.	organic virgin coconut oil
2 t.	organic grade B maple syrup (optional)
1 c.	raw cacao nibs, for garnish

Yields: 4 popsicles

Directions:

1. *Make the popsicles*: combine ingredients in a blender and blend on high until combined, about 60 seconds. Pour into popsicle molds and freeze 4+ hours to set.
2. *Make the dip*: combine chopped cacao paste, coconut oil, and maple syrup in a small saucepan over medium low heat and cook until chocolate is melted, about 3-5 minutes. Remove from heat and let cool.
3. *To assemble*: have a parchment-lined tray ready. Pour Chocolate Dip into a narrow-mouthed cup, wide and deep enough to fit the popsicles. Pour the cacao nibs onto a wide platter in an even layer.
4. Un-mold the frozen popsicles. One by one, dip into the chocolate, then roll through the nibs. Place finished popsicles onto the parchment-lined platter and place them back in the freezer for 5-10 minutes before serving.

CHOCOLATE CRUNCH POPSICLES

SWISS SNACK ROLLS

A childhood favorite made wholesome and grain-free. Moist, deep chocolate cake is rolled together with coconut cream filling and bathed in a thin chocolate syrup.

Yields: 4 large rolls

Chocolate Glaze

4 oz.	100% cacao paste/liquor, chopped
2 T.	organic virgin coconut oil
2 t.	organic grade B maple syrup

Cream Filling

2 c.	organic full-fat coconut milk
1/4 c.	filtered water
1 T.	grass-fed gelatin
2 t.	organic grade B maple syrup
1 t.	vanilla extract

Chocolate Cake

4 oz.	100% cacao paste/liquor, chopped		3	pastured eggs
1/3 c.	organic grade B maple syrup		1 t.	vanilla extract
1 t.	blackstrap molasses		1/2 t.	sea salt
3 T.	organic virgin coconut oil, plus more for greasing		3 T.	organic coconut flour
1 T.	raw cacao powder		1/4 t.	baking soda
1/4 c.	filtered water		2-4 t.	tapioca starch, for dusting

Directions:

1. *Make the cake*: combine chopped cacao paste, maple syrup, molasses, coconut oil, cacao powder, and water in a medium saucepan. Cook over medium low heat, whisking until chocolate is melted.

2. Preheat the oven to 350F. Line a half sheet pan with parchment and grease well with coconut oil.

3. In the bowl of a stand mixer, combine eggs, vanilla, and sea salt. Mix on medium speed until smooth. With the mixer on low, slowly drizzle in the melted chocolate mixture. Turn the mixer up to medium to combine, about 60 seconds. Add the coconut flour and baking soda. Mix another 60 seconds, or until smooth. Pour mixture into lined sheet pan. Bake 8-10 minutes, until the center is set (do not overcook, it will make the cake more prone to cracking when rolled).

4. While the cake is cooking, lie out a sheet of parchment (sized just larger than the sheet pan) on a clean surface. Dust with tapioca starch to cover the parchment in a thin layer to prevent sticking. Once the cake is cooked, immediately invert it onto the dusted parchment, aiming to line the long side of the cake with the edge of the parchment. Leave the parchment (stuck to the cake from the baking process) on the cake and roll the cake into a tight roll lengthwise. Set carefully onto a cooking rack and allow to cool for 45 minutes.

5. *Make the cream filling*: combine the coconut milk, water, gelatin, and maple syrup in a small saucepan. Cook over medium low heat until gelatin is dissolved, whisking continuously. Pour the mixture into the bowl of a stand mixer and place the bowl into the fridge for 30 minutes to cool.

6. Remove the chilled filling and place back on the stand mixer. Add the vanilla and whisk on high speed for 1-2 minutes, or until mixture is smooth and creamy. *(Note: filling may need to be mixed again immediately before spreading onto cake.)*

7. *Make the glaze*: combine all glaze ingredients in a small saucepan over medium low heat and cook until chocolate is melted, about 3-5 minutes. Set aside.

8. *Assemble the rolls*: very slowly unroll the cooled cake and remove the top layer of parchment. It may crack but don't fret, any cracks will be covered by the Chocolate Glaze. Spread the Cream Filling onto the cake in an thin, even layer. Roll the cake back up as tightly as possible, using the lower layer of parchment to help tighten as you roll. Secure with the parchment and move the roll into the refrigerator for 1+ hours to set.

9. Line a half sheet pan with a clean sheet of parchment. Remove the chilled roll and unwrap the parchment. Cut into 4 equal pieces (or more, as desired). Carefully dip each piece in the Chocolate Glaze and move to the parchment-lined pan. Work quickly to dip the remaining three rolls. Chill the rolls 10+ minutes before serving.

BAKED CHURROS WITH...

Chocolate Hazelnut Sauce

1 c.	blanched hazelnuts, soaked 8+ hrs
2 oz.	100% cacao paste/liquor, chopped
2 T.	organic grade B maple syrup
2 T.	filtered water
1 T.	organic coconut milk
1/8 t.	instant espresso powder
1/2 t.	vanilla extract

Baked Churros

2 t.	filtered water
2 T.	grass-fed butter or virgin coconut oil
1/4 t.	sea salt
2 t.	raw honey
1 c.	blanched almond flour
3/4 c.	tapioca starch
1 t.	vanilla extract
1	pastured egg
2-3 T.	grass-fed butter or virgin coconut oil, melted
1/2 c.	organic coconut sugar
1 t.	ground cinnamon

Yields: 12-16 churros

Directions:

1. *Make the sauce*: combine chopped cacao paste, maple syrup, water, coconut milk, espresso powder, and vanilla extract in a double boiler set to medium low heat. Whisk until chocolate is melted and mixture is smooth.

2. Place hazelnuts into the bowl of a large food processor and process until a smooth paste forms (this will take a couple of minutes, be patient!). Add in the warmed chocolate mixture and process to fully combine, scraping down the sides every 30 seconds or so. Serve with baked churros, as desired.

3. Preheat oven to 325F. Have a parchment-lined baking sheet ready.

4. *Make the churros*: melt water, butter, sea salt, and honey in a small saucepan over medium low heat. Add almond flour and tapioca starch, mixing vigorously. Continue to mix until dough forms a ball and pulls from the sides of the pan.

5. Pour the dough into the bowl of a stand mixer. Beat on medium speed until dough cools and there is no longer steam rising from the bowl. Add the egg and vanilla extract and beat on high speed until combined, scraping the bowl occasionally. Dough should be thick and very sticky.

6. Scoop dough into a zip-top bag fitted with a coupler and large fluted piping tip (optional, churros can be piped without a tip). Secure the bag shut tightly (with an elastic fastener, if possible) and pipe churros to desired length. Bake 20-25 minutes, or until just barely golden.

7. While churros are baking, place melted butter in a shallow dish wide enough to fit the churros. In a separate bowl of the same width, combine coconut sugar and ground cinnamon.

8. When churros are finish baking, immediately dip in butter, then into the sugar/cinnamon mixture. Shake excess off and place back onto the baking sheet to let rest 5 minutes. Enjoy immediately with Chocolate Hazelnut Sauce, as desired.

...CHOCOLATE HAZELNUT SAUCE

Enjoy this fun street food in the comfort of your own home.

BROWNED-BUTTER PUMPKIN ICE CREAM

The sweet and spicy toasted pecans bring out the nutty browned butter flavor in this pumpkin ice cream. Can be made without sweetener for a sugar free treat (pictured on pg. 56).

Browned Butter Pumpkin Ice Cream

1/4 lb.	grass-fed butter (1 stick)
1 can	organic full-fat coconut milk
1 15-oz can	organic pumpkin puree
1 T.	vanilla extract
1/2 c.	organic grade B maple syrup (or 1 c. Date Paste, pg. 40)
2 T.	brandy (optional to promote creaminess)
1 T.	ground cinnamon
1/4 t.	ground cloves
	pinch sea salt

Spicy Candied Pecans

2 c.	raw pecan halves
2 T.	organic grade B maple syrup (optional)
2 T.	avocado oil
1 t.	vanilla extract
2 T.	ground cinnamon
1/8 t.	ground cloves
1/8 t.	ground cayenne pepper
1/2 t.	sea salt

Directions:

1. *Brown the butter*: melt butter in a small skillet over medium-low heat. Continue to cook (butter will bubble) until butter turns a deep brown color. It should not smell burnt. Remove from heat and let cool to room temperature.

2. *Make the ice cream*: Combine coconut milk, pumpkin puree, vanilla extract, maple syrup, brandy, cinnamon, cloves, sea salt, and cooled browned butter in a large high-powered blender. Blend on high speed until mixture is smooth. Pour into a bowl and chill 4+ hours before processing in your ice cream maker.

3. Once chilled, process according to your ice cream maker's instructions. Move to the freezer for 2+ hours before serving. Serve with Candied Pecans, as desired.

4. *Make the candied pecans*: preheat 325F. Line a half-sheet pan with parchment or a silpat mat.

5. Whisk together maple syrup, avocado oil, vanilla extract, cinnamon, cloves, cayenne, and sea salt in a large bowl. Toss in pecans and mix well. Spread onto parchment-lined sheet pan and bake 20-25 minutes, tossing 2-3 times throughout the cook time. Remove and let cool to room temperature and break apart. Serve with ice cream or enjoy on alone as a sweet snack.

Note: can --sub Pumpkin Pie Spice for the cinnamon and cloves in the Spicy Candied Pecans.

APPENDIX:

RECOMMENDED SOURCES FOR INGREDIENTS

Almond butter, raw: a paste made from almonds that have not been roasted; **Artisana**

Almond flour, blanched: almonds that have skins removed and then ground very finely, gluten-free; **Honeyville**

Avocado oil: an oil high in monounsaturated fats with a high smoke point, great for baking at high temperatures; **Chosen Foods**

Blackstrap molasses: a dark syrup made from the maximum extraction of raw sugar cane, containing high amounts of vitamins and minerals; **Wholesome Sweeteners**

Butter, grass-fed: butter made from the milk of pastured cows, unpasteurized and unhomogenized; **Kerrigold**

Cacao liquor/paste, 100%: pure cocoa mass made by grinding cacao nibs with a higher amount of cacao butter than typically found in the average chocolate bar (sugar-free); **Navitas Naturals**

Cacao nibs, raw: the extraction of pure cacao solids cut into small bits, there is no cacao butter in this product; **Navitas Naturals**

Cacao powder, raw: cacao nibs which have been ground into a fine powder; **Navitas Naturals**

Chia seeds: a species of flowering plant in the mint family, packed with omega-3, fiber, antioxidants, and protein; **Chosen Foods**

Chocolate chips, mini: dairy, soy, and gluten-free dark chocolate made with cacao liquor, cacao butter, and cane juice; **Enjoy Life**

Coconut butter: a solid paste obtained from the flesh of the coconut, it contains both coconut solids and coconut oil; **Artisana**

Coconut cream: can be obtained by allowing a can of coconut milk to separate in the fridge and removing just the top portion, **Thai Kitchen**; or from purchasing pure 100% coconut cream, **Let's Do...Organic**

Coconut flour: ground from dried defatted coconut meat, high in fiber and gluten-fee; **Bob's Red Mill**

Coconut oil, virgin: oil that has been cold-pressed from fresh coconut meat; **Nutiva**

Coconut sugar: sugar produced from sap of flowers on the coconut plant, nutrient and fiber dense; **Wholesome Sweeteners**

Eggs, pastured: eggs from chickens raised in open fields, fed with non-GMO, soy-free feed; **Tropical Traditions**

Flaxseed, ground: a ground seed high in omega-3, lignans, and fiber; **Bob's Red Mill**

Gelatin, grass-fed: water-soluble protein made from collagen of pastured cows, hormone and antibiotic-free; **Great Lakes**

Honey, raw: unheated, unpasteurized, unprocessed honey straight from the extractor; **Wholesome Sweeteners**

Hibiscus flowers: dried flowers with a sweet, floral aroma; **Mountain Rose Herbs**

Maca powder, raw: a powder ground from the maca root, high in B vitamins and a natural source of energy; **Navitas Naturals**

Tapioca starch: a starchy, white powder made from the cassava root; **Let's Do...Organic**

Vanilla powder: sugar- and alcohol-free powder made with vanilla extract; **Nielson-Massey Vanillas**

INDEX

Made in the USA
San Bernardino, CA
07 March 2014